EN ROUTE TO THE EMERALD CITY

EN ROUTE TO THE EMERALD CITY

Chris Valli

RANA PRESS ● LONG BEACH, CALIFORNIA

EN ROUTE TO THE EMERALD CITY
Published by The Rana Press
45 Sea Isle Drive
Long Beach, California

Book Production by PCV Photographic Services
Santa Monica, California

ISBN 0-9651414-0-3
Library of Congress Catalog Card Number: 96-092162

Printed in the United States of America
By Modernage, Los Angeles, CA

In Memory
of
My Mother

CONTENTS

Acknowledgments

At this time I wish to express my appreciation to my children, who were a constant source of encouragement during these past seventeen years while I put my musings to print.

I would also like to thank my husband who brought me back to reality one day so long ago. After rescuing our four children from playing in the evening traffic, he came in, stepped over my lifeless body where I lay reciting my mantra, and said, "Life's not that difficult ... what's for dinner."

PREFACE

Regardless of the era in which we inhabit this world of ours, there comes the day in every parent's life when they realize, "My child is beyond the age of reasoning."

There is also the harsh reality that you don't have the answers to the really big questions in life—the questions concerning the greater scheme of things.

While we were totally submerged in the turmoil of daily existence—trying to deal with the complexities of our radically changing society, by instinct and guesswork, our children outgrew us.

Now what ...

These unsophisticated, unworldly children have been exposed to a world beyond all comprehension—never again to breeze through childhood with the security of "white lies" and guardian angels ...

Do we leave this problem to the theologians, philosophers, the dedicated people in the scientific world, our government, or do we become involved citizens and work within our local communities to alleviate some of the social ills in THIS life, before we search for the true meaning of EXISTENCE?

— Chris Valli
January 14, 1996

Chapter I

Sunday Morning Mass

The time is eight-twenty-nine. The year is
1977. The flowers look beautiful and the candles are glowing. The altar boy appears and
places the cruets in the proper spot—adding the
finishing touches in preparation for the celebration of mass. It is eight-thirty and the organist
sounds the proper chords, hailing the arrival of
our priest at the altar, signaling the warning to
be in your pew and silent. The organist reduces
the volume to a holy processional tone. The first
altar boy approaches, carrying the cross, fol-
lowed by the chalice bearing officiate for today's
Eucharistic service.

The usual feeling of "sanctuary" and inner
quiet that settles in after a hectic week, while

relaxing in the pew, just isn't there today. It has been an insane past hour gathering everyone up for the drive to church and maneuvering for the best view of the altar. It is our son's first mass and I am hoping he doesn't stumble and toss the big heavy, red prayer book onto the elderly priest's feet. I am also concerned that the back of his hair looks like the Alfalfa character of "The Little Rascals" series.

It is eight-thirty-five and all of the actors are in place—the service begins and still no tripping or funny faces at the boys in the front pew. He seems to be in a more somber mood this morning. Relaxing, I tune into the happenings around me. The congregation is rising and I hear the familiar strains of ...

"A mighty fortress is our God. A bulwark never failing.

Protecting us with staff and rod, His power all prevailing.

What if the nations rage and surging seas rampage.

What though the mountains fall, the Lord is God of all.

On earth is not His equal.

GREETING

In the name of the Father, and of the Son,

and of the Holy Spirit.

AMEN...

The grace of our Lord Jesus Christ and the love of God
and the fellowship of the Holy Spirit be with you all.

AND ALSO WITH YOU..."

As I am slowly being lulled into my usual
Sunday calm, I glance up at "our" altar boy. I
notice an expression I have never witnessed
before. Is it a spiritual thought he is having, is
he receiving a special blessing, has he forgotten
what his next duty is, or is he just plain bored?
Whatever, I am off again. Could this twelve year
old that we brought into the world be asking,
"Where are we coming from, why are we here,
and where are we going?" If he should ask me,
what will I say? Do I have any answers? He is
beyond the seven year age of reasoning theory
and he has the Baltimore Catechism questions
and answers on religious doctrine etched in his
brain.

"Who made me?

God made me.

Why did God make me?

To know him,

To love him,

and to serve him..."

I cannot insult his intelligence with pat answers or insulate him like my mother did me when I was a five year old, waking in the night worried about growing old, or asking if I have to die. Her resolute, "No, you don't have to die and you don't have to grow old," let us both go back to sleep, and at the same time, kept me happy for several more years. I had so many fun things to do. If my mother had turned on the lights, made a pot of tea, and brought in the Bible, the effect would have been nightmares for weeks.

Perhaps our son has had some all-knowing friends, like my Lutheran friend, Elaine, who told me there was no Santa Claus. But she also informed me that we wouldn't have to eat liver in heaven. Elaine also taught me a bedtime prayer,

> "When at night I go to sleep
>
> fourteen angels round me keep..."

Although I continued to recite my old, "If I should die before I wake..." prayer, I somehow felt more secure because now I had a vivid picture of fourteen angels crowding out the ever-present pictures that changed every night as to how I might die before morning.

With little crutches along the way, I was able to make it through those early years when we are the most impressionable—so maybe I am worrying unnecessarily. But that was in the

1930's. What about now? Will this little altar
boy be as comfortable with death without the
experience that I had with my Catholic friend,
Nancy, at the age of eight or nine when we
spent a whole summer finding dead birds to
bury in our chicken wire fenced bird graveyard?
Again, a worldly friend taught me to wrap the
birds in satin before we buried them in their
"very own" graves adorned with cross, stones,
flowers, and prayers. While we went about our
grave digging and attending to our mortuary
duties, Nancy told me about miracles and
saints, something we had never heard of in our
weekly Sunday school classes at the Methodist
church, thus further strengthening my childhood faith.

Regardless of the new concepts in what the
young can handle, a mother knows when a child
is too young for the truth....

THERE ARE NO ANSWERS.

Let him ride out blind faith a little longer.
How else could this young person do the job
ahead of him this year—serving at funeral
masses, seeing and feeling the grief of those left
behind? Let him hear the comforting advice the
priest will give to the bereaved.

We are standing again.

PROFESSION OF FAITH

"We believe in one God.

The Father, the almighty.

Maker of heaven and earth.

Of all that is seen and unseen.

We believe in one Lord, Jesus Christ..."

Until this moment I have always believed, or rather, I have never thought about it for more than a fleeting moment.

"We believe in one holy Catholic

and apostolic church.

We acknowledge one baptism

for the forgiveness of sins.

We look for the resurrection of

the dead.

And the life of the world to come.

AMEN."

Yes, it is nice and comforting to believe there is life after death, but that takes a lot of believing.

Is this my "safe place" because of so many years of blind faith, or is it habit? Do I question my faith today because now it is my turn to guide those around me? I may be called upon to attest by those I am responsible for—those I have promised to raise as Christians. Could it be the ritual, the music, the fellowship, or the Saturday confession—a ritual that enables you to seek guidance in the little or big complexities of daily life? It worked for me in the fifties, but would it have been enough to keep the parents and teenagers of the sixties and seventies off the so-called analyst's couch.

Do I do it for myself or has Sunday mass been something we all do for our children so they may have something to fall back on in their hour of need? Do we do it because our parents gave us a chance at religion as young children?

If questions do arise, how does one give guidance without diluting any of the teachings of the church or any of the building blocks for a philosophy of life that may have been acquired from church or home and dealt with in the mind of a child?

Why should they be worrying about answering questions that not even the most learned persons have been able to answer...?

"Deliver us, Lord, from every evil and grant us peace in our day. In your mercy keep us free from sin and protect us from all anxiety as we wait in joyful hope for the coming of our savior, Jesus Christ..."

Drifting off again...

I know why I am here today—because of our children. Why are the others here? Actually, where are the children? Where are the young adults and the younger families?

Have we scared them off with perfection, the one true church, original sin, or was it the changing times?

Maybe it was just plain rebellion, a little muscle flexing, a normal part of growing up, and some testing of both the authorities at home and church. But coming on the heels of the repercussions from the sixties, reverberating through every area of our lives, we parents and the clergy, regardless of our religious beliefs, panicked. It was the first time around for all of us and we lost our confidence, as well as our unity—all of us going in different directions trying to do our best in virgin territories.

All of our values were being questioned: a passage of time that would have lasted a few months in the fifties with maybe some glum family dinners, but we would have been in control—our children would have benefited because of our consistencies. We all would have been right in line with the Doctor Spocks of that day.

ORGAN SOLO

SILENT PRAYER....

Do only the elderly or the sick attend mass these days? Are they giving thanks, seeking divine protection, or is it fear of breaking one of the precepts of the church? Maybe they are lucky and still have blind faith....

CONCLUDING RITE

PONTIFICAL BLESSING

"Blessed be the name of the Lord
NOW AND FOREVER
Our help is in the Lord
WHO MADE HEAVEN AND EARTH
May almighty God bless you,
In the name of the Father and of the Son, and
the Holy Spirit...."

Are we any closer to revealing the absolute truths and meaning of existence?

Would Goethe still feel the need to put his thoughts to poetry by creating a fictional laboratory for Faust, who would sell his soul to the devil for just one more chance to find the true meaning of life, after having failed to do so during a lifetime of dedication to this cause?

Have we come any closer during our century — closer to the Bible accounts of Genesis — a moment of creation with the perfect balance of materials to allow the creation and nurturing of life?

"Holy God, we praise thy name.
Lord of all we bow before thee
All in heaven above adore thee,

EN ROUTE TO THE EMERALD CITY

Infinite thy vast domain
Everlasting is thy reign
Infinite thy vast domain....

The mass is ended. Go in Peace."

Chapter II

In the Land of Oz

So we "go in peace"... Just how long will the peace last? If we are lucky it will no doubt last until around 8:15 a.m. Monday morning. Then, its out in the "cruel, cruel world" without Auntie Em.

Will Monday be any different than it was for children in the Medieval days? Their thoughts and anxieties being drowned out by the babble of the country people selling their vegetables, cattle lowing, peddlers hawking their wares, farmers gaping at the jugglers, or rich merchants exposing the guildsmen to the handsome trappings of the rich. Maybe they would see a knight along the way and with luck a king or queen. Not to mention the ever present thieves making their way through the crowd looking for victims whose valuables could be snatched in an instant. Maybe a group of pilgrims enroute to Jerusalem would arouse the inner longings of the young to see what's out there—pilgrims who were too impatient to even prepare or know how far or where their dreams might in reality take them. They sought the Holy City at all costs, believing in the same healing shrines or doing penance as believers of today. But, as always, we will hope for a day that is a more fictional, dreamy one with the Wizard of Oz munchkins and good witches helping them along the yellow brick road, bolstering their courage with happy music in preparation for the scary times.

Happy music may have worked in the fifties, and maybe now and then in the sixties or seventies, but today in the nineties they will be lucky if they make it to school without getting gunned down or raped. Once secure in the relatively safe confines of the school grounds they will have to be on the lookout for the bullies that might take their lunch money or homework answers. Or, maybe the nineties' bullies would be more like the Mighty Morphin Power Rangers. The bell will sound and assuming everyone arrived intact, and it wasn't necessary to call 911 or a SWAT team, the morning will begin with some cheery remarks.

What then in the travel through life? All of

the road signs that you will not see on the way to the Emerald City will begin to appear. These signs will be more frightening than the "Big, Bad Wolf" or "Where the Wild Things Are." In fact, in our overly warned society the warnings will be more on a par with:

> "Now I lay me down to sleep
> If I should die before I wake
> I pray the Lord my soul to take."

The lessons of the nineties will include the death of furry animals, acid rain, save the seals, save the spotted owl, and don't forget the elephants—Oh yes, your daddy might die if he smokes, maybe even this evening—and, also pesticides. Now, if you are older, say ten or eleven, and can handle the heavy duty stuff, you will hear about racism first, the holocaust, nuclear bombs, and death with dignity for the eighth graders, a little about hazardous waste and global warming. The most shocking and most eminent will be that the German doctor in 1868 was wrong when he said that our normal body temperature is 98.6—actually, today's research tells us our normal reading could be as high as 99.9. If this one doesn't shock the students it certainly will shake up the dear old moms. But it really doesn't matter because most of it will fall on deaf ears, as there will be other distractions.

Several eyes will be on the bulge in the pocket of the boy in the green jacket because the butt of a gun is visible. The observers will be hoping this "angel" will either ditch school soon, or not be in the vicinity of the toilets. They already know that a locker mate has a knife and that is why they are carrying every book needed for today's classes on their backs.

Although Monday is a school day, it will be pretty much the same as Sunday mass—a learning experience—a time of growth and an important stage of development. The one difference being, while attending mass the young people were not put in any immediate danger of death or injury, even though the occasion left them with the feeling that the wicked old wizard was just hanging out in the Emerald City waiting to dispense punishment on those who cross a certain line.

The lunch hour will be a change of pace, a breath of fresh air, time to blow off any of the morning's morbid messages. Some will toss the apple in the trash but they will not feel the least bit guilty today because they have just learned about apples being saturated with dangerous chemicals. The big question will be, what to do with the gummy white bread sandwich laden with moldy carcinogenic peanut butter that also has trans fatty acids from hydrogenation. And, heaven knows what they do to us. Some will actually nibble their sandwiches and then very kindly share the remainder with a "friend" that wasn't in the same horror class. Meanwhile, many of the other students will be casting wary eyes skyward to see if any acid rain is about to consume them.

Lunch break over, they are in for a real treat. One of the priests will speak during the religion period. He will answer their questions pretty much like a priest in any period of time and the students will be as confused as Dorothy was when the munchkins and the good witch enlightened her in the Wizard of Oz.

"At the East, not far from here", said one,

there is a great desert, and none could live to cross it."

"It is the same at the South", said another.

"For I have been there and seen it.

The South is the country of the Quadleings."

"I am told", said a third man, "that it is the same at the West.

And that country,. where the Winkies of the West live,

is ruled by the wicked witch of the West,

who would make you her slave if you passed her way."

"The North is my home", said the old lady,

"and its edge is the same great desert

that surrounds this land of Oz."

Was the only option the yellow brick road when L. Frank Baum wrote his first book, <u>The Wonderful Wizard of Oz</u>, in 1900? Was he saying the yellow brick road was the only way or the easiest way?

When children have questions, maybe it is simple answers they seek, nothing beyond finding Auntie Em and Toto—with only personal insecurities concerning their immediate future, it may not be necessary to clutter things up with heaven and hell and original sin.

After making it through the school hours the real challenges surface after 3:00 p.m.. The decision-making has been up to either the parents or the teachers but now what will each child have to deal with once they leave the protection of their teachers. If you have a parent or care-giver at home you can zoom home with fewer options. Depending on your age you may be pretty much on your own for the next few hours. If you are a latch-key child or a young person whose safety and temporary guidance has been entrusted to a less than perfect adult, the challenges will be more complicated.

If you are one of the underprivileged children in the nineteen-nineties, you really don't have many choices. Your goal will be to make it home without being noticed by the ultimate bullies— the gangbangers. You might hang around the playground as long as possible, or if you're lucky, you will be able to run to the shelter of the local Boys and Girls Club. Maybe a school chum will invite you home or you might have a birthday party invitation—an invitation that you will have to refuse because you will not have a way home even if you could buy a gift.

But what will happen to the more privileged boys and girls—the boys and girls with the so-called traditional family with a stay-at-home parent, a 3:30 p.m. mom, or some semblance of a full-time family? Will they be any better off physically or emotionally? The boys will have the toughest time because they are already pegged as complicated, hard to manage and everyone wants to shape their future.

These children, whether boys or girls, will be programmed for the next three hours with all of the many lessons, lectures, and cultural outings that money can buy. If they do have a day off now and then, would they "dare" go home and watch TV with the possibility of becoming a couch potato hanging over their heads? Heaven forbid! Would they chance lying on their bed to stare out the window and watch the clouds roll by while listening to a little music? Could they possibly enjoy a snack that's fat-free with no sugar or salt added?

Auntie Em is still down in that cellar and even though she is peeking out a knot hole in the cellar door—while screaming out with all of her accumulated wisdom—she cannot be heard because of all of the interference from the darn wind...Auntie Em doesn't understand the look of shame on Dorothy's young face. Dorothy, who compared to her classmates, is way ahead in the "curve" department. "...and what are those boys saying...Poor child, she hasn't done anything to be ashamed of...Oh my! Why are those tall girls chasing the short boys...Stop, stop, stop!"

For the middle America children with a parent at home, those of the so-called lucky kids who will get to their "safe place" hours before the evening meal, the unloading process will be over so mom or dad can walk into a relatively calm situation—a 1950's traditional family with a few modifications. They will have blown off Monday and for that matter also Sunday, looking forward to Tuesday. Maybe months will go by before they have a soul-searching thought, and the boys will be honoring some of the other girls with cat-calls and nasty name calling.

In the dining rooms across America the characters will be different, but the end result will be the same. Dinner will not be that relaxing, they all know the script and have learned how to handle family dinner. The dialogue that the moms or dads have to resort to has to be one that is quick, brief, and to the point, not unlike the conversations during their work day. The narrow window they are allowed with their children doesn't allow for any children faking choking or dropping of silverware when they don't have the answers—if all of the "partakers" are to be addressed.

Unfortunately, the dinner hour coincides with the parents' re-entry into the home atmosphere. Because of Mom and Dad's own personal turmoil, it isn't always possible for them to pick up on all of the nuances going on between child and the respective parent, sibling rivalry, and any undercurrents between each other. But even on the best of days, the physical needs will take precedence over the emotional, while either mom or dad is trying to play catch-up, as well as keep the parental duties of "nurturing" on line in the areas of the development of character. The milk will continue to spill, the phone will ring, and the puppies will yelp, not to mention a few other distractions.

Many of the emotional hurts, real or imagined, that slip by at dinner may or may not surface during "the children's hour". Some of this mental anguish will linger and fester depending on just how urgent the parents' need is to get to their "safe place" on any given day. But, all in all, the same evening confusion of the 90's will not be much different than the 50's in regards to the child nurturing and the effect on the children. What will be slightly different is now we not only have the "original" lonely father—a father of the traditional 1950's or 1960's era—but we have a career mother, a mother that is not always working because of a financial need, as in the simpler days (not that this is bad). It's just the new way...

Nevertheless, while these career women try to keep up with the demands of today's society, their genes are pulling them in all directions—another lonely person.

At least the original lonely person, man, was born to be lonely because he was the sole provider, protector, mentor, and head of the household...

A MAN'S HOME WAS HIS CASTLE..

Chapter III
Lonely People

We never did know what the 50's father's "real" day was like. Even if they had been able to stay awake, we would not have known because these men had been programmed since childhood to keep a stiff upper lip, set a good example, keep your emotions under control, and never burden others with your problems. And especially, do not concern your wife with your anxieties regarding keeping a roof over the family's head, along with food or clothing need nightmares. These were the same attributes that enabled the young men and women of the 1940's to emotionally survive World War II. They were serving God and country with dignity.

The hope of going home to rebuild the country they were defending—a country put on hold—is what got them through many a night in foxholes. They had vivid pictures in their minds of the wife and children they would have when and if they made it back to the States. Promises to God were also made if they did indeed survive...

Yes, it all happened eventually, for the lucky ones. Our country was reborn. There was a new growth and prosperity. The goals and horizons of the American male had expanded beyond belief. There were enough opportunities to go around twice for everyone in America in those days. The self-discipline that made them good soldiers allowed them to create the architecture of the post-World War II expansion. These servicemen kept their promises to God and the fifties gave birth to the years of the churchgoing traditional family.

And then came the 60's. What a devastating blow to these World War II fathers when reality set in—all of the plans for the new free country written off to greed. Written off to greed not by other countries or scholars, but by the very children they nurtured. And the flower children told them what REAL LOVE WAS, while chanting GOD IS DEAD. The euphoria was over—in just one generation. What they had fought for did not last long enough for their grandchildren to enjoy the fruits of the American dream.

After some thirty-five years, these same

flower children have a hunger and thirst for a spiritual life. A psychic phenomenon is sweeping the nation—people looking for a "happening". If they hear a board squeak, it is a message from beyond... People from all walks of life caught up in miracles, mysteries, and myth mania. Many are looking for a "quick fix" religion or solutions to whatever torments their souls, while others are very methodical in a search for spiritual meaning. Whatever name it goes by at this point, it is spiritual gluttony.

Like so many other endeavors of this middle-aged group, when they want something it is no holds barred, there is no stopping them. An analogy could be made between the excessive behavior in both the quest for the perfect body and the need for a spiritual life—something beyond themselves. When the aerobic dancing, tai chi, tofu, and ginseng didn't give them the inner tranquillity they were looking for, they realized the necessity for something that would help them understand and accept their inner struggles. As George Will wrote sometime ago, "Health, like any wealth, can be pursued too ardently and hoarded too greedily. Wise grandmothers know you should not try to maximize anything."

When this modern-day group of pilgrims began their first pilgrimage in the 1960's, they too were as impatient to reach their destination as the medieval pilgrims had been—only they did not have an actual city in mind or a route to follow. Our sixties group of humanity had one "goal" and that was to break with tradition—the slogan was "down with the establishment", with no defined plan.

Perhaps it was just fear of serving in Vietnam, and "just" a little bit of idealism, or were they trying to shed a conscience that had been developed slowly since their childhood? And, then again, it could have been what some of us liked to believe—our enemies were infiltrating our college campuses. Whatever the reasons, it was a period when America lost a great deal of its moral bearings, a time when the family unit was declared optional.

The increased use of drugs, by adults and children, was sending shock waves through every corner of our society. When the college campus drug users rattled our cages thirty-five years ago, we were up in arms because our perfect little children were being touched by the fallout. We had our little PTA lectures and there were many enthusiastic citizens who momentarily stirred to action, but when it took more than cocktail party talk they fell by the wayside. We were displaying the same apathetic behavior in those early years of the Vietnam war until one day we walked to our postboxes and retrieved our copies of <u>Time Magazine</u> with the cover story of a naked little girl running down a street trying to escape her burning back—a day when many of us finally realized Vietnam was a real war...

The protests continued and the causes multiplied. It was a loud voice echoing through our peaceful existence, spilling over to the 1970's, with a huge influence in lifestyle changes.

The seventies were, more or less, the birth of feminism. The young women wanted the right to act like men. But, somehow during this upheaval the tables turned. Men and women were no longer partners in causes, they were angry adversaries. Not every young woman had a three hundred pound father that left them alone to care for a sick mother, as did Gloria Steinem, but they all were able to dredge up comparisons.

Being a housewife was reduced to scrubbing toilets and baking cookies, causing a mass exodus of women from the bungalows of America. These women were the young and the brave with no need of man or God.

This movement was not because of a financial need. They were not trapped in physically dangerous marriages, nor were they unhappy drudges, any more than they were bored chocolate eating "lovenovel addicts". Many of these women left their homes reluctantly and only because the changing of the status from housewife to homemaker didn't stop the feminist eyebrows from rising when they were told, "Only a housewife." They left to justify their existence in the eyes of the feminists, so as not to be characterized as leeches on society.

It was not a smooth journey. There was confusion and resentment, with very little support from the home front. The husbands viewed this effort, the "giant step" for women's rights, as working for fun and little more than a monkey-wrench in their personal income tax brackets.

There were many lonely people in those days, not only women and men, but the third person in the traditional family triangle—the lonely child, convinced that the problems between his parents would not be, were it not for his existence. These children were not only growing up in a family where the parents were experimenting with new lifestyles, but also without the benefit of a belief in a guardian angel, the storybook version of baby Jesus, and heaven to help them when the "family fear" syndrome set in.

When Baum wrote one of his later Oz books, The Magic of Oz, in 1919, just after World War I, his dedication read,

> "To the children of our
>
> soldiers, the Americans
>
> and their allies, with
>
> unmeasured pride
>
> and affection."

We forgot to give our Vietnam veterans a feeling of pride and we certainly were stingy with our affection. We filed "war" in a back drawer of our minds and in the minds of our children. Patriotism was dead. The post-Vietnam children were growing up without the morning flag salute, no patriotic music, and without a morning school prayer.

Since those early days of the two career family it has been almost impossible to understand what the effect has been on the children. Whether it is negative or positive, we will never hear it vocalized by the younger members of the family. At least the adults have, or should have, the skills to deal with the pressures confronting them, even though they do not always use these resources when the mental turmoil sets in.

These parents were not heartless, uncaring, self-absorbed individuals. They were aware of the behavioral changes in their children and they did try to compensate for the anxieties that they were introducing into the family unit. But, because of the sudden and accelerated pace while they were experiencing new lifestyles, it was not possible to meet the needs of each family member. There were also external forces influencing each family. It was the first time around for everyone concerned and the meager supply of analysts' couches from a happier day could not handle the overload or stem the rising number of lonely people.

While the anti-establishment members were filtering back into the mainstream, they didn't exactly roll over and die. They still had their causes, with a big influence on the minds of the young people. These causes were more of an apocalyptic nature. Although the apocalyptic messages have toned down some with the fall of communism, the threat of Bambi's mother being killed in the forest is still a major worry for youngsters, not to mention the slaughter-houses that put the hamburgers on their MacDonalds trays. Children are being frightened in areas that should be their down-home, apple pie "safe place".

Before we can come to any conclusions about a new and different kind of loneliness, we have to wonder where each one of us fits into the individual, not so new, lifestyles of his or her family and their support system. We must also not underestimate the influence that the surrounding community affects our lives no matter how diligent we are at home . On one hand we have children growing up scared, living in drug infested neighborhoods with gang warfare and juvenile homicides both at their doorsteps and on the school grounds. Their parents hide behind high fences, barred windows, and make-shift alarm systems. On the other hand, we have the overly programmed child growing up in relatively secure surroundings, but growing up aggressive, meeting their parents' expectations at all costs with very little respect for their peers. They are the products of parents trying to produce a "super child", one who excels in everything. In general, these are overwhelmed children who know better than to make any waves.

In either case, there is a widespread fear about public safety. As one writer put it, "Something precious has gone out of American culture, and we don't know how to get it back."

For a variety of reasons we see many lonely people in our 1990's age of anxiety. It is not the Ellis Island lonely feeling that the 1800's immigrants experienced when they had landed in America, saying good-bye to their homeland, to begin a new life. These immigrants had hopes and dreams to carry them forward. Nor could it be compared to John Steinbeck's <u>Grapes of Wrath</u> "Okies" of the great depression. These victims of bank foreclosures, traveling with whatever they could manage in their rattle-trap vehicles, had a place to go, an out. They were able to physically escape from the life of destitution that they were being faced with in the Midwest. There was the "hope" of the land of milk and honey. It didn't work out for everyone. It took hard work and set-backs, but it was possible.

As we muddle through to the next millennium, our entire nation is being touched by violence, an over-taxed social service system, and a different kind of loneliness—a feeling of hopelessness for many, and for others, an overwhelming feeling of where and how to begin the reconstruction of America.

While some are seeking spiritual answers, our nation's politicians, community leaders, and philanthropic organizations are vying for a position that will enable them to score a victory in the race to cure the ills of our modern-day society.

During the jockeying around period, will the cast of characters that represent the violence, poverty, and victims of abuse and neglect be satisfied with hearing "It is God's will", "Suffer now and great will be your rewards in heaven"? "Have no fear", "If God cares for the birds in the fields why would he not care for you?"...

As we continue to search for solutions, the historical events of our century, or any of the most recent centuries, really don't matter. There will always be fallout of some kind. Who in a million years would believe that while we were focusing on social issues, science, through technology, was continuing at such a rapid pace, that George Orwell's "telescreen" warnings regarding the horrors of an electronically controlled universe in his novel, <u>1984</u>, would come so close to a reality by producing a 1996 latch-key kid—at home, with all of the dead bolts in place, needing to be warned of the on-line pedophiles in the age of cyberspace child abuse.

Certainly, a different kind of loneliness...

Chapter IV

In the Beginning...

In the beginning, God created heaven and earth, and in just seven days, while allowing for a designated day of rest. Or was it a single giant explosion that gave birth to the cosmos—the Big Bang theory, a theory that has been going on since 1912... For now this theory seems to be getting top billing and it doesn't conflict with the Bible's account of Genesis. At this moment in time our top physicists insist the "Big Bang" has no rival when it comes to explaining fundamental aspects of the universe.

Does this current evidence of mathematical hard facts and assumptions help any of us in our own spiritual journey, or enable us to guide our children with a new degree of confidence?

Even if some of us have received reassuring answers, we are still faced with original sin and heaven and hell—a vision of the black angels being cast out of heaven with such force they penetrated the earth to its fiery core, to reside in the dominion of the devil for all eternity—and still no Adam and Eve...

Mankind has certainly benefited from the scientific advancements of all ages, even though we are, more or less, at a standstill with the Big Bang announcement. Unless some of the diehards continue their research, they haven't solved the riddles of the heavens, and they haven't got any closer to understanding the mind of God that some genius of today had hoped to do. Science has been able to control disease, pain, death for many people, and given us many physical comforts. They have blessed us with medical breakthroughs from aspirin to lung transplants. However, they have relegated us to one big "equation", with our only hope being, if we do vanish down a big black hole, there is a possibility we will surface every few billion years. But how many of us give any thought to the dimensions of time and space beyond a clock, a calendar, or our own domain? And, if we did, could we even understand the theories being presented these days?

Is this a hopeless scenario, or should we view this knowledge as a matter of the "wonderful wizard" just playing hide-and-seek with the scientist, and go on our merry way, believing in miracles—the miracles of a religious life, as opposed to the areas of physical science's unexplained phenomena? Is it time for us to move on and stop trying to understand religion through science?

Before we resign ourselves to "blind faith" we still have a chance with the famous Leakey family, who along with their many colleagues, have dedicated their lives to the research of the origins of mankind's physical, social, and cultural development. Perhaps they will find Adam and Eve as they continue their discoveries which have been gradually changing the profile of our original ancestors to one of a larger skulled, wiser and taller man walking upright with a free striding gait, and actually having heels, toes, and arches similar to our own. Could it be possible that the gap in time, immediately following the Big Bang, that is troubling our theoretical physicists, might be solved by anthropologists rather than by astronomers...

While our lives do depend on the present day technology that gave us spaceships to the moon, commercial air travel, airborne warfare, and the computer that launched the information revolution, very few of us understand the actual principles involved in the creation of these scientific "monsters" any more than we understand the creation of man or the biological evolution of man. Most of us are still waiting for Darwin's dream to be fulfilled, that a complete theory, his or anyone else's, would be discovered and understood by everyone, philosophers, scientists, and ordinary people.

Whether the theologians, philosophers, or the many dedicated and capable people within the scientific world unravel the mysteries of the universe, or if the many involved citizens in our government and local communities are successful in alleviating some of our social problems, we cannot turn back the clocks to a more innocent, less informed universe in the hope of recapturing a more peaceful existence. We cannot abolish scientific research, smash our laboratories, or go back to nuts and berries and the bacteria laden compost.

Einstein once wrote to a colleague, "I would not think that philosophy and reason itself will be man's guide in the foreseeable future; however, they will remain the most beautiful sanctuary they have always been for the select."

Perhaps we will be lucky and the continuing battle between religion and science, that has been simmering ever since the ecclesiastical authorities of Rome were threatened by Galileo's scientific discoveries (supporting Nicolaus Copernicus' fifteenth century theory that planets orbit the sun), will reach a truce before the end of our century. Then science can be taught as science, and religion can be taught as religion— without science proving God and religion proving miracles.

For now, we have an eager group to address— souls, to either win over or welcome back. How do we begin the long trek back to the churchgoing days of the past. And, how do we recapture the sanctuary of Sunday mass or Saturday temple? Do we kill a fatted calf, prepare a feast, and celebrate the return of the sons and daughters of the 60's? And, do we say "all is well" and pick up where we left off when religion was put on hold...

Have we learned anything from those days of the empty church pews? Will the clergy of the multitude of religions rush out with opened arms to claim their fair share of souls searching for a spiritual life, proclaiming the advantages of whatever religious denomination they represent. In our own enthusiasm as parents and grandparents will we be broadminded and patient enough to let them lay their own foundation that will enable them to accept a religious life in the nineties—a religion of their choice.

Will it be possible for us to stand by without shouting out with self-righteous advice and at the same time avoid the hypocrisies we were accused of...?

Maybe, once again it is worrying unnecessarily. If the children of the sixties have realized that something is missing in their lives they certainly have come to the conclusion that leading a religious life is more than attending weekly services and reciting a few daily prayers.

They have exhausted the sects and occult, but are they ready to give up the "East"? If they find peace and serenity in the practice of monastic solitude, will it be another detour from the mainstream of life in the country of their birth? Can they afford the luxury of a life of a Tibetan monk when our communities are crumbling around us at a time when they are needed to share their knowledge, capabilities and the energy of youth, to rebuild America for our future generations?

Hopefully, they will choose a way that fosters a community lifestyle and a reaching out to all of society. They are too young to accept a life of eternal bliss "before" the grave—a returning to dust and nature before it is necessary—or one that might encourage laziness because they have decided to embrace a power beyond themselves, and, be content to rely on this power for their life's existence.

While they map a route for one of the most important journeys they will ever undertake, will they be able to control their emotions and not be overwhelmed by the myriad of New Age religious material that is available to anyone looking for spiritual direction in the 1990's? Will they be able to keep a strong head and form their own conclusions when they encounter the overly zealous along the way? Will they realize what is right for one person is not necessarily the way for everyone and sometimes not even a long term or sound way—possibly only a Band-Aid?

It will be very simple to accept the mathematical truths of science. But there will only be blind faith for those who choose a spiritual life. Despite the rift between the medieval scientists who were banned from continuing their research by the Roman Catholic church (which was at the same time fending off the Protestant reformation), science has continued to flourish for almost five hundred years, bringing it to its present day status which is light-years from the laboratory of the fictitious Dr. Faust. Even though God didn't disclose his whereabouts, there is no disputing the positive results of centuries of scientific achievement.

Unlike science, religion is the same as it has always been. Scholars keep up their constant efforts to disprove Jesus and the Bible, and Christianity in general, but the believers continue... Even when the young fifteenth century, Roman Catholic monk, Martin Luther, defied the Holy Roman Emperor, he was not trying to change Christianity, but to restore what had been lost during the long years of the church's endeavors to survive. As with all of the established religions, whether it be Judaism, Christianity, or Islam, they have survived throughout the ages and without the benefit of proven mathematical facts.

Although we have not come any closer to the true meaning of life, we have time on our side—centuries of believers content with blind faith. Truly, in the words of the reformation hymn, "a mighty fortress is our God. A bulwark never failing...on earth is not His equal." Not everyone is fortunate enough to arrive at "blind faith" with only a desire for faith. For many it is a never ending journey, like the medieval alchemists on their quest for the philosophers' stone—the unknown substance that might perfect the human soul, while also enabling them to transform base metals into gold. As we near the end of our century, maybe we have made progress—we no longer search for the elixir of the soul in science...

Chapter V

After "Physics"

How do we, as laymen, survive spiritually following our attempt to find answers through the
laws of physics? If we are not one of the "select"
that can find a holiness in the "wonder" of the
infinity of the cosmos, and we do not think and
speculate on the very highest intellectual levels
as the philosophers and the Einsteins of the
world, where do we go from here?

For those of us who are still committed to
finding believable explanations for our children
and grandchildren, do we retreat into a state of
meditation? Do we hold our breath in anticipation of a supernatural happening, or do we suggest the life of an atheist with only the dismal
outlook of nothing beyond the grave? These

options do not offer any conclusions, and certainly are not very helpful.

In retrospect, it was naive of me to believe that I needed to provide concrete answers. Maybe it was enough to pack their lunches, drive them to school and let them find guidance through the Catholic church. It has been fifteen or twenty years since the first time I experienced any self doubt concerning my ability to give spiritual guidance to anyone beyond the age of reasoning. Although I did make feeble attempts from time to time, my lack of conviction was so evident, the subject was usually dropped and I just listened. Thank heavens the questions that were put to me seldom went beyond arguments regarding the validity of the Catholic church and their own guilt feelings experienced while being pressured to accept and live by the teachings of the "one true church" while coming of age in a rapidly changing world. Fortunately, I was never put in the position of actually having to "attest" regarding my sincerity when reciting the numerous creeds and confessions of faith that have allowed the Catholic church to maintain a continuity and identity.

On some occasions, these interrogation sessions had a striking resemblance to the uncertainty experienced by the young priest, Martin Luther, before he naively set out to enlighten Rome. After years of wearing a hair shirt, and fearing damnation by a judgmental father in heaven for his imagined and overly exaggerated sinful ways, he vented his anger on the church with accusations of the hierarchy having failed to feed the faithful in the indispensable word of God. In Luther's mind, he envisioned the "Freedom of a Christian" as a personal relationship with God, instead of reliance on works elaborate in ritual and dogma—in general, questioning "authority" as do our children of today.

When the youth of America questioned authority during the destructive sixties and they declared GOD DEAD, their declarations went beyond the United States' involvement in Vietnam, abolishing the establishment, or rebelling against the unquestioning demand for obedience to the laws of the established religions of their parents. They violated the rite of passage allowed the "idealistic years" of young adulthood during any generation, with parental "perfectionism" bearing the brunt of the attacks.

Were it not for the Vietnam War, this normal period of intellectual development that also coincides with the shedding of the shackles of ones' teen years, we would not have had a full-blown war on our home front. These actions set off a chain of events that is just now being broken in the nineties. As the dust continues to settle the spiritual renewal taking place has everyone running helter-skelter in an attempt to recapture those innocent years of childhood blind faith.

Why has is taken so long to regain our equilibrium? It has been some thirty or thirty-five years since the radical young adults of America had their struggles with God and religion—when they took issue with our government—and set out with determination to redefine the American value system.

When our country lost its post-World War II unity during the sixties and our religions began to falter, it was somewhat like Luther's early reformation years while attempting to restore the Roman Catholic church to its pristine beginnings, after having made his first visit to Rome as a young unworldly, but highly respected priest and teacher of theology at the University of Wittenberg. When he made this initial trip to Rome, having never witnessed the iniquities of life in a large city, he was ready to hold his superiors in Rome accountable for the failures of humanity.

A parallel could be drawn between the unsettling conduct of the Berkeley and Kent State radicals to the actions of the young Martin Luther. When these students passed judgment on our government's strategies in suppressing the forces of communism in Vietnam, their actions were comparable to the shortsighted, idealistic, explosive behavior toward the church, by the young Martin Luther. When his untimely arrival home from Rome landed him smack-dab in the middle of an All Souls Day celebration, he acted accordingly. What he encountered was an aggressive fundraising event taking place for the benefit of the Roman Catholic Church. On this occasion the dressing for success power dressers of Rome were orchestrating the dispensing of indulgences that might free loved ones' souls from purgatory in exchange for "monetary contributions." The amazing results of the highly charged atmosphere on that fateful day some five hundred years ago tells us what a single, head-strong youth can accomplish.

Whether it be the protesting youth of our present-day sixties or Luther's in the fifteenth century, who chose to challenge the authority of the church of Rome, the outcome is the same. When Luther either ignored or distorted the efforts of the church in their endeavors to raise the status of the church of Rome in Europe from one of grungy sandalled monks in rough-hewn robes to one of credibility and power, little did he realize he would shatter the church he loved and served. The schism caused by his actions continues to this day.

When our judgmental youths' actions sent a strong signal of a division within the ranks of our government, they too had disregarded the explanations of their parents and the more mature population of America. There was total indifference to the fact that the Russian and Chinese communists might join forces with their counterparts in North Vietnam, with the possibilities of touching off a more critical world situation. They gave little thought to the fact that there might be a well established, ambitious communistic network working within our country. This dissension sent out a strong signal of "weakness" in America. Rather than stopping the war with their inexhaustible energy, they actually prolonged it, giving it the distinction of being the longest in our history.

There is no doubt that these past thirty-five years of turmoil have had a devastating effect on the lives of everyone in America, but, isn't it time to give up our differences and start the healing process that is so long overdue? What a wonderful day it would be if suddenly we stopped flip-flopping between romanticizing or condemning those long ago events of Vietnam. Although the children of our most recent generations were not part of the Vietnam era, there has been a long lasting impact on their lives in more areas than religion.

Unlike the sixties that have left many Americans confused and lonely, the reformation years were not the cause of a breaking down of communities, and there was no concern that God might be dead. They still had a unity of sorts and the blind faith of a god-fearing medieval mind with the family unit still intact.

Now Mr. Wizard where do we go from here...

In looking beyond the more immediate problems of today, how do we address this present day search for spiritual roots? Is it possible for any of us to help this group find a firmer footing on which to build a solid religious life? Do we sit by passively and risk the possibility of blowing it the second time around, or do we get actively involved? Hopefully these thirty-or forty-something children of ours will be more receptive to our religious views after having done it their way. They just might listen if we tread lightly and resist the urge to pontificate with the pat answers of the laureates.

The more prudent way to go might be to sit by silently in the hope that these "mature" adults, because of their strong desire to return to the flock, will reap the benefits of the formal religious training of long ago...

Another suggestion might be for us to concentrate our efforts on a more tricky element of nurturing—the challenge of creating an innocent childhood blind faith for our younger members of today's society—a faith they might have had, had they been born in less complicated times.

Having missed out on the conditioning years of white lies, baby Jesus stories, and an early introduction to guardian angels, these young people will not accept our explanations as readily as the pre-age of reasoning children will.

Again, where do we begin?

After having lost some credibility in the eyes of the day-care crowd when we lied about Santa Claus, it does appear to be a next to impossible task.

Somehow it is difficult to picture the cyberspace super-child of the nineties, the ultimate couch potato (suffering from carpal-tunnel syndrome) tapped into his fingertip knowledge of Internet, being the least bit impressed with grandmotherly advice.

Fortunately, American commercialism, with its handy-dandy master calendar of the traditional religious holidays, has been able to keep the myths of the major religions alive.

Surely there were mumbled half-truths uttered during the merriment of opening gifts and the holiday feasting with loved ones, that might have given the children a "glimpse" of the teachings of a man called Jesus. Perhaps there was a wise person now and again that gave them a quick recitation of the Golden Rule—"do unto others as you would have them do unto you". There might have been times when Moses and the ten commandments entered into the festivities (minus the burning bush). Both accounts being uncomplicated, acceptable guidelines for a way of life, while at the same time offering an explanation for the widespread participation in religious holiday celebrations. We could leave well enough alone at this point. This might be the time to take a temporary detour from the Bible.

The Star Wars approach might be the way to capture the attention of the science fiction set when we take a stab at defining either evolution or creation.

They most certainly would not relate to our parents' analogies of our being an ant or a cog in a wheel in relation to the vastness of the universe. These children would rather speak in terms of being an "infinitesimal speck in time" and immediately launch into an attack on our disrespect for the world we inhabit. After all, anyone who believes in God couldn't possibly care about anything but the human soul.

We cannot depend on a blending of philosophy and religious beliefs when we are addressing the future Theoretical Scientists of the world—stifling the chances of producing an "Einstein" that might discover the "true" meaning of our existence. We cannot discourage them before they have a chance to explore the cosmos with the machines of the next millennium.

Assuming we are able to stumble through the fundamentals with some degree of success, how will we approach the "real" questions—death—

and the prospects of dying without white lies and blind faith? Even if we have been able to offer a small amount of comfort about the here-after, we are still faced with setting an example, with some semblance of order, in our own behavior and thought processes as we attempt to guide them in their continuing search for answers.

This could be an unnecessary effort. In fact, these super-children may have already come to the conclusions that it is more important to deal with the more immediate paranoia that is gripping our society—the business of living rather than dying being a top priority—and not waste precious time on earth with what lies beyond the grave.

Scholars tell us that "rapid scientific changes in technology have altered our lives so radically, that the Bible's accounts of Genesis seem irrelevant."

Regardless of the spiritual state or the physical dangers being experienced by individuals in the nineties, we do have to send out a message of hope...we have a powerful nation that is number one, and thanks to the research of modern-day paleontologists, the endangered world is not as endangered as the doomsayers would have us believe. If we could get these two messages across to the young ones during the formative years, we might do more good during this period of emotional development, than pushing too far, too fast with blind faith.

This is not to say "exclude our heavenly father", but to enforce confidence and encourage ingenuity in adolescents and young adults as they deal with the stressful events of today's society.

Rather than offering the false hope of the proclamations being made by the Bible-toting politicians of America, we need to join forces with the less political clergy of the traditional religions who have said "stop the name calling and support those who advocate a conscientious real dialogue between different constituencies with legitimate concerns and a gospel of love which can bring people together."

Some good advice has been offered to us by the priest, Father Henri Nouwen, who has taught theology at several of our more prestigious universities. He suggests in his book, Reaching Out, a three point plan. One, of understanding ourselves first; next, reaching out to others; and ultimately a relationship with God— as we go down our paths to spirituality. This is not a bad plan for a beginning when we all go out in force to rectify the errors we made while trying to understand the rapid changes in our society in recent years.

As we continue to fantasize, we could very well put God on hold a little longer and apply Father Nouwen's advice in response to the frenzy that surrounds us during this modern-day renaissance. A call to arms has been sounded throughout America with the threat of a re-enactment of the Medieval power struggle between papacy and the Holy Roman emperors, occurring sometime in the future, if we buy into the present Christian Coalition's contract with the American Family.

It might be better for each one of us to examine our personal conscience in relationship to the people in our own local habitat. If we press the fact that our world has expanded beyond simple solutions and the pat answers of our Sunday school lessons, it would be a start in the right direction. There is no one cure for the ills effecting our world population. If we pray at all it should be for leaders who will contribute to the laying down of a firm footing for constructing an up-to-date *world* infrastructure that will continue well into the next millennium.

Have we accidentally stumbled into one of God's five-hundred year plans that he is continually fine-tuning in readiness for the day when we sink so low that we have nowhere to turn but to him...

If Martin Luther was able to successfully challenge the mightiest power on earth in his day, the Roman Catholic Church, and pull off Protestantism with only a primitive form of moveable-type—think what might be accomplished on the cyberspace superhighway—as we go careening into the year 2,000...

Chapter VI

The "Reeling" World

Before we can travel beyond this all-time low point in our topsy-turvy society, we need to unload a heap of excess baggage.

The wailing and weeping has to stop. It is time to stop beating our chests and moaning "Dear God, why?" At some point in time we need to stop the fantasizing and move on. Until we stop perpetuating hatred by living in the past, we will never recapture the post-World War II days of a stability that was attributed to a predictability in the behavior of others.

It is time to stop fighting the most recent wars of our century every time there is a twenty, thirty, or fifty year celebration of the "END" of these conflicts. For every accolade bestowed on a hero, there is lamenting over a multitude of atrocities that took place during the war years.

There are many outstanding museums along with tons of war archives available for future generations, without the daily reminders on TV or radio, and in the periodicals that are creating a negative influence on the present day youth of our nation...

It is not necessary to prove that a new age was born after World War II. Nor is it right to continue the guilt trips we have been hanging on the radical youth of the sixties. As painful as the memories of the indignities of war may be, we cannot live in the dark recesses of the past and expect a radiant future.

What is the solution?

Although baring the soul is in vogue these days, surely the answer is not to have unnecessary shallow confessions by our past leaders, with little consideration that they might be adding fuel to the dying embers of the memories of war—while in pursuit of salvation before they meet the grim-reaper.

Our lives, whether laymen or one of the body of elected officials, are being saturated with the daily batings of the political talk show hosts— with their followers hanging on every word and then gleefully relating the profound thoughts of the day to anyone that will listen. The ranting and raving by the articulate TV personalities who have outlived their refreshing beginnings, can't be the answer...

For those of us who were never in the political arena, other than campaigning or voting for the candidate of our choice, our worldly responsibilities rarely went beyond those we faced at breakfast and also tucked in at bedtime.

How do we atone for past omissions?

Perhaps our fifties traditional family was plastic in some respects—as we were told in no uncertain terms by the women who came out of the woodwork to support the feminist movement. The happy and contented never spoke out. We slinked away and meekly defended our position.

Unless we were actually confronted by a gung-ho friend or neighbor, we kept a low profile. We continued to diligently fulfill our commitment of preserving the traditional family infrastructure—which was in no way a death sentence.

Many of us who made the projected twenty year "housewife" commitment at age twenty-three or twenty-four, in the mid-fifties, that has ultimately turned out to be forty years, might say these years spent with our families were rewarding, spiritual, fun-filled, romantic years. A period of time to be cherished above any other choices we might have made. But that would be a little less than honest...

What could be said in all honesty is that we all have our own personal regrets of one kind or another. The number one regret agreed on by a large majority might be that we didn't have the courage of our convictions when our values were being attacked.

Our biggest complaint would be the loss we experienced during the decline of the caring community network that supported us in the early years. When the very fabric of our existence was being ripped to shreds we buckled under to the pressure of the feminist movement, not realizing we had a much stronger force in our camp—we had men...

A regret or fault of equal consequence was our lack of religious conviction that allowed us to be swept up with the tide when our churches were declared antiquated. We lost faith and struck out on our own when our main source of strength was being accused of lacking the immediacy necessary to provide any real assistance in coping with contemporary social problems.

We allowed ourselves to be affected by the skepticism of a skeptical age—we forgot our younger days of idealism and the second thoughts we had in regard to traditional commitments before we became preoccupied with the business of living.

As the American family lifestyle continues to change, the task of rebuilding our communities becomes more and more staggering. If we are to relieve the climate of fear that has people of all ages living nervously from one moment to the next, it is evident that we need to start with our government. If we are to achieve any real and lasting reform in the US of A, we of the citizenry of America have to appeal, in a non-violent way, to our elected officials to set aside their overly aggressive political ambitions during this time of re-evaluation that is taking place in our land of plenty...

Now that our next presidential race is on, we should ask our candidates to remember the moral and social responsibilities that we all must live by if we are to regain our caring community networks. We must, at the same time, remind ourselves that an X in the proper ballot box will not give us an immediate magical, painless end to the social ills besieging us at the end of this century.

We might also remind ourselves that even with all the "troops" in tow, we of the rank and file will still have our own individual consciences to deal with.

The stumbling blocks that we will encounter along the way will not be insurmountable if we all do our part. We cannot go on blaming our government, or others, for every mishap that befalls us along the way to the Emerald City of our hopes and dreams—where we will find the answers to eternal peace...

Although we have been successful in eliminating some of the crushing problems of the early part of this century such as poor sewer systems, infant mortality, disease, illiteracy, sweatshops, and the elimination of the dreaded orphanages of the depression years, we are still left with street gangs, slum lords, violence, and drug cartels operating freely at our borders.

As we near the end of this century, our biggest challenge will be the reclaiming of our children. The most pressing questions will be how do we restore the innocence of childhood? Once they have been exposed to mindless violence and have witnessed disrespect for human life, is there any chance of regaining those beautiful carefree years that all children are entitled to?

What will it take to wipe out the images of the sordid side of life? Will they be able to block out the sounds of the street vulgarities of the nineties? And, what about the young people who may even have lost their own self-respect?

We have gone beyond "boys will be boys" in our age of children wielding deadly weapons, or the old truancy days of the fishing hole and smoking corn silk behind the barn. Nowadays, ditching school covers a wide range from parental approval when a baby sitter is needed at home, to off campus lunches with sex or drugs that deaden any enthusiasm for afternoon classes.

Assuming we are successful in re-establishing

community support systems, will there ever be a time when children from all walks of life will have an opportunity and desire to be molded into good citizens who will become role models for future generations?

In reflecting on how we might recreate a schoolroom with an atmosphere of learning free from fear of bodily harm, or without threats of impending crises that will destroy our earth...where do we start?

It is very difficult to imagine a nineties child—who has been brainwashed since pre-school of the possibilities that humans are endangering every life form from tadpoles to grizzly bears—in a fourth grade classroom of a simpler era. They would be bored to death with our big gray linen geography book. It would appall them to know that the students of bygone days were as intrigued with the physical creation of their books as with the contents. Even more shocking would be the "no-brainer" attitude concerning the value of a schoolbook over dead fish in the brown water close by the paper mill. They would no doubt heave a sigh of relief and with a cautious smile stand a little taller when they heard our confident explanation regarding bombs. They might also nod their heads in agreement when we told them with authority that bombs saved lives and stopped wars.

With the frightening environmental information available today, it would be extremely difficult for a youngster to comprehend the necessity of cutting down trees to enable the construction of homes, schools, and churches. It would be equally amazing for them to know the long history of the reforestation programs in our world.

Has anyone told them of Teddy Roosevelt's concerns for the ecosystem, or the Alexander Humboldts and John Muirs of their great-grandparents' day... There has always been concern for the conservation of our natural resources, the ecosystems, and the threat of war. But the lessons in our schools were of a healthy, respectful, thankful nature, without extremes and black clouds of doom floating overhead. The worries and physical actions to protect us from the devastation of war or the depletion of our ozone layer was the work of adults...

These well-versed "child" environmentalists would never be satisfied with the simple heaven after death explanation—they will never bury a dead bird knowing about mites, plague, and some birds being blind because of a depleted ozone layer. When they study mass extinctions down through the ages it will never be a gradual process due to ice-ages or volcanic action. Neither will they be caused by an asteroid impact—unless it is qualified by too many humans and global warming.

The earth sensing satellites that relay daily global conditions via the latest computer technology are eons away from the barometric devices that we were in awe of at a tender age. For the first time in the history of mankind it is possible to calculate global temperature trends that could cause a global warming (if and when) that might equal a "nuclear winter." Scary and possible, but how probable...

Our "endangered earth" is over and beyond "war" or any of the other dire warnings the youngsters of today are faced with when they eagerly board that big yellow school bus on their first adventure away from mommy, daddy, or nanny.

If all of the above-mentioned could be set aside, would educators, parents, and family support systems have half a chance to focus on helping children build a sense of character? Is it at all possible in an age when peers or TV stars rank number one in choices of role models?

It will be easy to train acceptable behavior for the times when parents or teachers are present. The real trick will be to shape their minds and personalities so they will react in a kind, responsible manner when they are on their own.

The next question will be how to guide these budding personalities when we offer daily input as we aid them in developing a conscience free from guilt, shame, resentment, or fear? How many people, programs, churches, or schools will it take to mold one "good" citizen?

In contemplating how and who might be the best choices for tackling this unharnessed power that is our present generation—isn't it time, for us of the pre-World War II days, to relinquish the reins to the generation of survivors—the baby boomers?

Regardless of their radical beginnings, there are highly qualified people in all walks of life willing to step in to access and remedy our modern-day complexities. These middle-aged citizens have grown up during our society's progressively deteriorating years. It is only reasonable that these rudderless nineties youth be guided by the preceding generation that is more in touch with today's values and hidden demons.

The gap between our pre-sixties parenting that included the "Father Knows Best" mentality or Sid Caesar/Imogene Coca humor and "Saturday Night Live", could never be narrowed enough to make a significant difference. While we fantasize about a return to the "Leave It To Beaver" or "Captain Kangaroo" TV viewing, our grandchildren are growing up with "Mighty Morphin Power Rangers" with an occasional glimpse of "Dirty Dancing."

If we think of the children and how they are faring, a case could be made that in any of the most recent decades parents have been poised to meet their children's every need. Although many have fallen through the cracks because of failed experimental social and educational programs, the consistencies of the long established non-profit community organizations have made a positive difference. The programs that have been individually geared for the particular problems of each area being served, appear to be very successful in saving a small number of the more vulnerable children.

Our communities have not been abandoned during these past few decades. Along with family service groups, church youth activities, and gang counseling, there has been a good effort, by the Catholic Church's educational system, to absorb the children of many under-privileged families.

Although these struggling caring networks have helped to lighten the load for a few people, they cannot continue or expand without financial assistance from our "cognitive elite" in Washington...

With everyone covering the trouble spots—where will the old folks fit in? There will be opportunities to make a meaningful contribution from time to time, but our most valuable message will have to be one of hope.

We might also make a difference if we lend children our support in a realistic way without a Pollyanna air, or set them up for disappointments by preaching the blind determination of "positive thinking"... And, we might also spare them some heartaches if we resist the temptation of heaping inordinate praise in an effort to build self-esteem.

Will anyone really thank us after their first reality check, when they are enlightened to the fact that the false praise and contrived opportunities were indeed detriments, when subtle, honest recognition for minor achievements would not only have built real self-esteem, but would also have fostered self-motivation.

In spite of the countless eleventh hour attempts to restore some order in the lives of our children and grandchildren, during the winding down of our century, the route will not be easy. Our one prayer should be that they not be victimized by information and misinformation that abounds in our age of statistics.

Violence and the more obvious examples of our society's ills are not the only threats to the well being of people of all ages in today's world. If our FDA and other government regulatory administrations can protect Americans from experimental medications, avant-garde medical procedures, and environmental hazards, why are we not shielded from the onslaught of statistical analysis. With the most recent in depth studies regarding intelligence and class structure, we are all being stereotyped and analyzed to death. Gone are the days of prenatal care, well balanced nutrition and the surviving of childhood illnesses that would ensure children growing in stature and self-confidence, an assurance that they might achieve the goals of their dreams and at the same time develop into law-abiding citizens.

We are being paralyzed by analysis. The research covers every avenue from bodily chemistry to IQ, race, cultural backgrounds, class distinctions, and last but not least—gender differences.

Ever since the early days of feminism, when women raised those angry fists in defiance of men, we have been inundated with studies centering around our changing moorings. It was only expected that scholars would rise to the occasion and come forth with ANSWERS...Many of the theories have been proved invalid and have been replaced with even more research. With all of the miscalculations, skewed statistics, and inconsistencies, it has been next to impossible to know the exact effect the lifestyle changes have had on our society.

As a critical, sometimes envious, and rarely sympathetic observer of the new lifestyle changes that have ignited the gender war, it is certainly clear to me and most lay people of my time, that unless we restore the delicate balance between men and women, our social problems will never go away. Until each person comes to terms with their inner struggles it will never be possible to reach out to family, friends, or community. And the lonely cycle will repeat itself...

The answers will never come from accumulated data with faulty conclusions or selectively controlled information that is ignored when it does not agree with the researchers point of view.

With the defining of gender roles still in a state of flux, many people are killing themselves trying to live up to the promises made to each other while they were still in the "courting" stage of their relationship. The days before the babies—or the business opportunities that might come their way with concentrated effort—were a reality...

When the wives and mothers of the seventies and early eighties rejoined the work force they were able to establish priorities when the family units stress level started to escalate. There is no turning back for the loving, caring parents of the nineties, and as in the past, parents are taking too much blame and too much credit for the failures or successes of their children.

Being a full-time present-day wife and mother includes the financial aspect of care-giving, as well as, attending to the daily physical and emotional needs of children and the elderly. While a large majority of today's parents strive to maintain a family unit that resembles one of the fifties, they are being immobilized with guilt because of the many areas in which they are unable to duplicate the revered "traditional" family—through no fault of their own. Should they really strive for a working relationship that is based on the choices or goals of a totally different era than the one in which they exist?

With the nineties norm of a two career family whose professions are of equal importance to the immediate and long term financial and psychological well being of all of the members of the household, there is no luxury of a full-time fifties helpmate in the home. Many relationships are crumbling under the burden that our fast paced society has placed on the shoulders of the new "superpeople". They feel trapped and exhausted, with no relief in sight. Gone are the candlelight dinners and the waiting slippers by the fireplace. These mellow evenings have been replaced with fast food and the much needed stress relieving workout at the gym, along with the necessary weekly therapist visit that keeps "it" together to a certain degree.

The burnout will continue unless the adult members of the family team are adept at recognizing each other's needs at any given time, as well as being willing to juggle personal schedules to lessen the stressful times. Any effort will help to relieve a certain amount of the daily trials and tribulations, but what about the deep-seated, more complex reasons for physical exhaustion?

For some women, the frustrations being experienced in the professional world when life does not bring them the satisfactions they aspired to, cannot be a whole lot different than the reverse situation that some of the super-moms of the post-World War II period strug-gled with when they felt exhausted and trapped within their four walls—burdened and abandoned by their dawn to dusk upwardly mobile husbands—who in either case may have jumped on the bandwagon for the wrong rea-sons or because of peer pressure.

If we think of how the men are faring since being released from the role of sole bread-win-ner, when they were forced to be unisex par-ents, we might make an observation that the men are doing okay at "mothering"...But it just isn't in their genes to flutter around a nest. They have not, thank heavens, been blessed with the inherent nature of the female to give 100% of her attention, 100% of the time. They were born to provide, protect, and to father—and to keep the delicate balance of nurturing in its proper perspective.

What the willingly involved new age fathers, who have not been victims of bad feminism, have had the pleasure of doing because of the more leisurely relationship with their children, is the opportunity to present an approachable non-authoritarian father figure—one who performs his disciplinarian duties but has time to stick around for the follow-up hugs and kisses.

But even in the seemingly contented house-holds, where all of the members appear to be making a smooth, orderly transition into the "new" traditional family unit of the twenty-first century, there are still doubts. If the parents of today could sit in the seat of a spectator at this twentieth century event, they would give up the doubts and guilt and enjoy life. The young families of today manage to have their evening outings to the yogurt shop, evening family video viewings, and storytelling. The parents are involved in the children's schools and they still help with homework. They still have the bed-side conversations in a darkened room, when the little ones get up the courage to tell mom or dad about the fears of their day. Yes, it may be 9:00 p.m. rather than 7:30 p.m., but the bottom line is they provide the same safe haven and those middle-class values that became the hallmark of the fifties. Hopefully, the therapists are coun-seling them in the same way as our Friday night confessors did—"Count your blessings, you are doing a better job than you think, you're not alone, you're trying too hard"—with five Hail Marys and one Our Father.

Another "safe haven" that has surfaced during this period of adaptation is the extended school year choice and after-care programs that are available in the better funded public schools. These programs are providing protection by qualified school staff members for children during the "wary hours" of 3:00 p.m. to 6:00 p.m., as well as allowing the youngsters an exposure to music and art along with the much needed after school playmates. Gone are the days of a mother, aunt, or grandmother in every home, and children frolicking as far as the eye can see. While the parents and children benefit, the grossly underpaid teachers have an opportunity to supplement their incomes.

Now, if the government could be enticed to redistribute funds from the ineffective, mismanaged, failed, money consuming programs...

With a little encouragement from the senior critics of the "new way" these liberated women (and men), with thirty years of struggles behind them, could continue the pioneer spirit and work out the remaining obstacles with fewer misgivings.

When the power plays, competing, and the who did what to whom, ceases in the home, there is a pretty good chance it might stop in the work place—and ultimately carry over to the community. If it *is* at all possible for men and women to see each other in a more favorable light, the undercurrents that fuel the gender war may fall by the wayside.

With only a few remaining roadblocks women can focus on the milestones achieved and rest on their laurels, secure in the knowledge that because of supportive men in their lives they have been freed of the stereotyping that has haunted them since childhood—and graciously accept the new lifestyle choices with their fewer social constraints.

With our communities being composed of many individuals and groups and our social rules and values having been greatly altered, it would be a strong force if women and men could now stand in agreement on values, standards of conduct, and the "rules of the game".

If we can assume that it is possible to restore the delicate balance between man and woman, and at the same time there is a sincere systematic attempt by our newly elected officials who promise to address the particular circumstances of life in our individual communities, this might be the time to go to stage three of Father Nouwen's plan when searching for spirituality—reaching out to God...

Chapter VII

The "Not So Magical" Answers

In this year nineteen-hundred and ninety-six, there is a captive audience waiting with bated breath for the one sound piece of evidence that might push them beyond skepticism to the realm of blind faith.

Theologians might do it...But they are at a disadvantage because in the end they have only blind faith to support their teachings. And scholars are doing a magnificent job of muddying everyone's thought process by putting a personal spin on the works of every philosopher that has ever lived, as well as filling their minds with present-day interpretations of the Bible. They have reduced the Bible to a collection of writings by a handful of folklorists and religious mystics who lived in the eastern Mediterranean two or three thousand years ago. With added guesswork there is also the implication that there was no such person as Jesus Christ. For those who have not been able to come up with concrete evidence that there was not a man called Jesus, the stories vary from his being an illiterate, spellbinding itinerant preacher to at most, possessing a healing touch on an emotional level only.

Regardless of the effort being made by the participants of such scholarly groups as The Jesus Seminar, to prove Jesus as nothing more than a mortal peasant, the fact remains that we are approaching the 2000th birthday of the man called Jesus— 2000 anno Domini...

Whether or not Christianity was a divine plan, it was founded on the teachings of a man called Jesus, and with only a handful of followers, a universal church was established.

We cannot deny the saturating effect Christianity has had on every aspect of man's activities from physics to politics, to the moral values that have caused such a stir down through the centuries. Since the beginning of time philosophers, musicians, poets, and artists have been absorbed with the well-being of man's soul and his eternal destination. Will he ascend into heaven to reside with the angels or tend the furnaces of hell?

It must also be remembered that the proponents of the theory of evolution are lurking in the forest ready to pounce on the weary travelers at any moment—with the "latest" mathematical findings...The information revolution will continue. Biotechnology will not go away. The industry that blossomed over forty years ago when Francis Crick and James Watson cracked the code for DNA, did nothing to substantiate Adam and Eve and has actually proved a need for an eleventh commandment: Thou shalt not recklessly perform the applications of genetic research on the human race.

During the "God is Dead" years the fear of the unknown—what lies beyond the grave—has certainly been the same as it has always been, but for those who have been deeply entrenched in the business of living, the need to comprehend the overall scheme of things, or the need of a spiritual life, has been overshadowed by concerns for one's daily existence. Their interests lie more in the area of the fictional negative utopias of Orwell and Huxley. Orwell's nineteen-forties warnings that "big brother is watching", if man continued to be automated, or the nineteen-thirties "Bottle Babies" of Huxley's, who were produced as a last resort to establish social order and stability in the world, were always considered pure fiction. However, warnings of despair—the powerless and hopelessness of modern man—is something many people prefer to identify with and are also able to live with, if they keep themselves busy enough...

Some of the lucky middle-aged people of today have evidently crossed an unknown threshold and are ready to continue exploring spirituality...

Again, Mr. Wizard, where and how?

However, demands for ANSWERS by the young adult students of theology and philosophy, who are just embarking on their journey into the unknown, go beyond the studies of cultural practices throughout history, or philosophical advice that will allow them to cope in today's society. They want answers to the true meaning of existence, and they want them now—they are not content to wait for the possible clairvoyance of old age.

They may be searching on their own now, but rest assured, these products of our electronic age will be by our bedside with all of the proper equipment in place—waiting to record every moment as we travel to the "great beyond". While they wait in anticipation for a glimpse of the other side, they will all have their own interpretations of our words as we croak out "Water, water!", so we might moisten our parched lips.

As the search continues they may even be led back to the church of their childhood. Although there are no concrete answers that will solve the mysteries of life, the way is strewn with concepts that need to be very closely examined if religious conflicts are to be avoided. A warning to steer clear of the beliefs and aspirations of others, while at the same time resisting the urge to convert fellow travelers, is certainly a harmless piece of advice.

Whether or not these travels bring them full circle to the faith of their childhood, before any faith can be embraced a close examination has to take place. The religions that have transcended boundaries of denomination, nationality, or time might be good avenues to pursue.

There is really very little anyone can do for another soul who is searching for inner peace— we can't possibly be faulted if we offer them choices and point them in the direction of the youngest of the world's major religions, Islam, whose teachings tell us man's only job is to surrender to God, Allah. Or, tell them of a Jewish woman's testimonial, "When Friday night comes we close our doors and light our candles, say our prayers, open our hearts, and then God comes in!"

If we suggest the life of Christ—a man whose impact on human lives looms larger than any other figure in world history—the road gets a little bumpy, because of the major ecclesiastical Christian offshoots since the reformation and Luther's excommunication.

However, in the words of our 264th pope,

Pope John Paul II, "We can understand that over the centuries Christ's message has been interpreted with varying emphasis. Good will is needed in order to realize how various ways of practicing faith can come together and complement each other."

As we near the 500th anniversary of the day in 1521 when Martin Luther fled the ecclesiastical authorities of Rome after having stated, "I cannot and will not recant."—perhaps John Paul II will find it in his heart to call for a present-day evaluation of Luther—with hopefully the same verdict of "not guilty," as was the result of the inquiry of Galileo. If a 17th century error can be rectified by the Catholic Church in the interest of a present-day understanding between science and the Church, why not a search, now, for the 15th Century issues of Luther in light of today's ecumenical goals— with a sincere dialogue, free from past obstacles, between the original culprits? This might be the time, while religion is in vogue, rather than waiting for a tearful heavenly embrace between Pope John Paul and Luther...

Although the dedicated theologians, historians and teachers have been able to preserve our religious roots, down through the centuries so we might survive the ebb and flow of mankind's religious fervor, they cannot go beyond their custodial duties of record keeping or performing the role of simplifying religious history.

Beyond catechism the way to blind faith for most people will be that one experience which cannot be explained away by the laws of nature—the one experience that will allow them to recite the creeds and professions of faith in a loud and clear voice from start to finish—with no hesitations or mumbling. At this point they will be able to confidently attest to "SOMETHING MORE" and continue with the same message of HOPE that our religious experiences enabled us to do.

In the end we will give guidance and support to our children and grandchildren that is similar to the instructions that the good witch of Oz gave Dorothy..."The road to the City of Emeralds is paved with yellow brick so you cannot miss it."

If we are asked if the WIZARD is a good man we will have to admit that we have not seen him. We will also say, "We cannot go with you but do not be afraid of him." Like the good witch we will use all of our magic arts to help them along the way.

Our own hope for the future will be that the religious dissenters of the past will be vindicated and excommunications lifted so we might have a reunited Christian church in the next century that is truly universal.

THE END